MW01715638

SRA

Open Court Reading

Ding Dong!

SRA

A Division of The McGraw-Hill Companies

Columbus, Ohio

www.sra4kids.com

SRA/McGraw-Hill

A Division of The **McGraw·Hill** *Companies*

Printed in the United States of America.

Send all inquiries to:
SRA/McGraw-Hill
8787 Orion Place
Columbus, OH 43240-4027

ISBN 0-07-569491-3
3 4 5 6 7 8 9 DBH 05 04 03 02

Ding dong! Ding dong!
Is that the bell?

It is spring.
Want to go swing?

Can I bring King?
He likes playing.

Let's fling a stick.
King will bring it back.

Fling that thing!
Fetch, King!

Ring! Ring!
Mom is ringing the dinner bell.
We cannot swing now.